Andrew Lang

Ballades and Verses Vain

Andrew Lang

Ballades and Verses Vain

ISBN/EAN: 9783742899675

Manufactured in Europe, USA, Canada, Australia, Japa

Cover: Foto ©Thomas Meinert / pixelio.de

Manufactured and distributed by brebook publishing software
(www.brebook.com)

Andrew Lang

Ballades and Verses Vain

BALLADES AND VERSES VAIN

BY

ANDREW LANG

AUTHOR OF "HELEN OF TROY"

"Branles, virelais, Ballades, and Verses vain."
—The Faerie Queene.

NEW-YORK
CHARLES SCRIBNER'S SONS
1884

CONTENTS.

iii

CONTENTS.

VERSES VAIN:

CONTENTS.

CONTENTS.

Laughter and song the poet brings,
And lends them form and gives them wings;
    Then sets his chirping squadron free
    To post at will by land or sea,
    And find their home, if that may be.

Laughter and song this poet, too,
O Western brothers, sends to you:
    With doubtful flight the darting train
    Have crossed the bleak Atlantic main,—
    Now warm them in your hearts again!
                 A. D.

Mr. Austin Dobson has been so kind as to superintend the making of the following selection from " Ballads and Lyrics of Old France" (1872), "Ballades in Blue China" (1880, 1881, 1883), and from verses previously unprinted or not collected.

viii

BALLADES.

BALLADE DEDICATORY.

TO

MRS. ELTON

OF WHITE STAUNTON.

— — —

T HE painted Briton built his mound,
  And left his celts and clay,
On yon fair slope of sunlit ground
That fronts your garden gay;
The Roman came, he bore the sway,
He bullied, bought, and sold,
Your fountain sweeps his works away
Beside your manor old!

But still his crumbling urns are found
Within the window-bay,
Where once he listened to the sound
That lulls you day by day; —
The sound of summer winds at play,
The noise of waters cold
To Yarty wandering on their way,
Beside your manor old!

The Roman fell: his firm-set bound
Became the Saxon's stay;
The bells made music all around
For monks in cloisters grey,
Till fled the monks in disarray
From their warm chantry's fold,
The Abbots slumber as they may,
Beside your manor old!

ENVOY.

Creeds, empires, peoples, all decay,
Down into darkness, rolled;
May life that 's fleet be sweet, I pray,
Beside your manor old!

BALLADE OF LITERARY FAME.

"All these for Fourpence."

OH, where are the endless Romances
  Our grandmothers used to adore?
The Knights with their helms and their lances,
Their shields and the favours they wore?
And the Monks with their magical lore?
They have passed to Oblivion and *Nox*,
They have fled to the shadowy shore,—
They are all in the Fourpenny Box!

And where the poetical fancies
Our fathers were fond of, of yore?
The lyric's melodious expanses,
The Epics in cantos a score?
They have been and are not: no more
Shall the shepherds drive silvery flocks,
Nor the ladies their long words deplore,—
They are all in the Fourpenny Box!

5

And the Music! The songs and the dances?
The tunes that Time may not restore?
And the tomes where Divinity prances?
And the pamphlets where Heretics roar?
They have ceased to be even a bore,—
The Divine, and the Sceptic who mocks,—
They are "cropped," they are "foxed" to the
    core,—
They are all in the Fourpenny Box!

ENVOY.

Suns beat on them; tempests downpour,
On the chest without cover or locks,
Where they lie by the Bookseller's door,—
They are *all* in the Fourpenny Box!

BALLADE OF BLUE CHINA.

THERE 'S a joy without canker or cark,
    There 's a pleasure eternally new,
'T is to gloat on the glaze and the mark
Of china that 's ancient and blue;
Unchipp'd, all the centuries through
It has pass'd, since the chime of it rang,
And they fashion'd it, figure and hue,
In the reign of the Emperor Hwang.

These dragons (their tails, you remark,
Into bunches of gillyflowers grew),—
When Noah came out of the ark,
Did these lie in wait for his crew?
They snorted, they snapp'd, and they slew,
They were mighty of fin and of fang,
And their portraits Celestials drew
In the reign of the Emperor Hwang.

7

Here 's a pot with a cot in a park,
In a park where the peach-blossoms blew,
Where the lovers eloped in the dark,
Lived, died, and were changed into two
Bright birds that eternally flew
Through the boughs of the may, as they sang;
'T is a tale was undoubtedly true
In the reign of the Emperor Hwang.

ENVOY.

Come, snarl at my ecstasies, do,
Kind critic; your "tongue has a tang,"
But—a sage never heeded a shrew
In the reign of the Emperor Hwang.

BALLADE OF THE BOOK-HUNTER.

IN torrid heats of late July,
  In March, beneath the bitter *bise*,
He book-hunts while the loungers fly,—
He book-hunts, though December freeze;
In breeches baggy at the knees,
And heedless of the public jeers,
For these, for these, he hoards his fees,—
Aldines, Bodonis, Elzevirs.

No dismal stall escapes his eye,
He turns o'er tomes of low degrees,
There soiled romanticists may lie,
Or Restoration comedies;
Each tract that flutters in the breeze
For him is charged with hopes and fears,
In mouldy novels fancy sees
Aldines, Bodonis, Elzevirs.

With restless eyes that peer and spy,
Sad eyes that heed not skies nor trees,
In dismal nooks he loves to pry,
Whose motto ever more is *Spes!*
But ah! the fabled treasure flees;
Grown rarer with the fleeting years,
In rich men's shelves they take their ease,—
Aldines, Bodonis, Elzevirs!

ENVOY.

Prince, all the things that tease and please,—
Fame, hope, wealth, kisses, cheers, and tears,
What are they but such toys as these —
Aldines, Bodonis, Elzevirs?

BALLADE TO THEOCRITUS, IN WINTER.

ἐσορῶν τὰν Σικελὰν ἐς ἇλα.
Id. viii. 56.

A H ! leave the smoke, the wealth, the roar
Of London, leave the bustling street,
For still, by the Sicilian shore,
The murmur of the Muse is sweet.
Still, still, the suns of summer greet
The mountain-grave of Helikè,
And shepherds still their songs repeat
Where breaks the blue Sicilian sea.

What though they worship Pan no more,
That guarded once the shepherd's seat,
They chatter of their rustic lore,
They watch the wind among the wheat:
Cicalas chirp, the young lambs bleat,
Where whispers pine to cypress tree;
They count the waves that idly beat
Where breaks the blue Sicilian sea.

11

Theocritus! thou canst restore
The pleasant years, and over-fleet;
With thee we live as men of yore,
We rest where running waters meet:
And then we turn unwilling feet
And seek the world — so must it be —
We may not linger in the heat
Where breaks the blue Sicilian sea!

ENVOY.

Master, — when rain, and snow, and sleet
And northern winds are wild, to thee
We come, we rest in thy retreat,
Where breaks the blue Sicilian sea!

VALENTINE IN FORM OF BALLADE.

THE soft wind from the south land sped,
He set his strength to blow,
From forests where Adonis bled,
And lily flowers a-row :
He crossed the straits like streams that flow,
The ocean dark as wine,
To my true love to whisper low,
To be your Valentine.

The Spring half-raised her drowsy head,
Besprent with drifted snow,
" I 'll send an April day," she said,
" To lands of wintry woe."
He came,— the winter's overthrow,—
With showers that sing and shine,
Pied daisies round your path to strow,
To be your Valentine.

13

Where sands of Egypt, swart and red,
'Neath suns Egyptian glow,
In places of the princely dead,
By the Nile's overflow,
The swallow preened her wings to go,
And for the North did pine,
And fain would brave the frost, her foe,
To be your Valentine.

ENVOY.

Spring, Swallow, South Wind, even so,
Their various voice combine;
But that they crave on *me* bestow,
To be your Valentine.

BALLADE OF SUMMER.

TO C. H. A.

WHEN strawberry pottles are common and cheap,
　　Ere elms be black, or limes be sere,
When midnight dances are murdering sleep,
Then comes in the sweet o' the year!
And far from Fleet street, far from here,
The Summer is Queen in the length of the land,
And moonlit nights they are soft and clear,
When fans for a penny are sold in the Strand!

When clamour that doves in the lindens keep
Mingles with musical plash of the weir,
Where drowned green tresses of crowsfoot creep,
Then comes in the sweet o' the year!
And better a crust and a beaker of beer,
With rose-hung hedges on either hand,
Than a palace in town and a prince's cheer,
When fans for a penny are sold in the Strand!

When big trout late in the twilight leap,
When cuckoo clamoureth far and near,
When glittering scythes in the hayfield reap,
Then comes in the sweet o' the year!
And it 's oh to sail, with the wind to steer,
While kine knee deep in the water stand,
On a Highland loch, on a Lowland mere,
When fans for a penny are sold in the Strand!

ENVOY.

Friend, with the fops, while we dawdle here,
Then comes in the sweet o' the year!
And the Summer runs out, like grains of sand,
When fans for a penny are sold in the Strand!

BALLADE OF AUTUMN.

WE built a castle in the air,
  In summer weather, you and I,
The wind and sun were in your hair,—
Gold hair against a sapphire sky:
When Autumn came, with leaves that fly
Before the storm, across the plain,
You fled from me, with scarce a sigh—
My Love returns no more again!

The windy lights of Autumn flare:
I watch the moonlit sails go by;
I marvel how men toil and fare,
The weary business that they ply!
Their voyaging is vanity,
And fairy gold is all their gain,
And all the winds of winter cry,
"My Love returns no more again!"

Here, in my castle of Despair,
I sit alone with memory;
The wind-fed wolf has left his lair,
To keep the outcast company.
The brooding owl he hoots hard by,
The hare shall kindle on thy hearth-stane,
The Rhymer's soothest prophecy,—*
My Love returns no more again!

ENVOY.

Lady, my home until I die
Is here, where youth and hope were slain;
They flit, the ghosts of our July,
My Love returns no more again!

* Thomas of Ercildoune.

BALLADE OF OLD PLAYS.

TO BRANDER MATTHEWS.

(Les Œuvres de Monsieur Molière. A Paris,
chez Louys Billaine, à la Palme.
1.D.C.LXVI.)

LA COUR.

WHEN these Old Plays were new, the King,
    Beside the Cardinal's chair,
Applauded, 'mid the courtly ring,
The verses of Molière;
Point-lace was then the only wear,
Old Corneille came to woo,
And bright Du Parc was young and fair,
When these Old Plays were new!

LA COMÉDIE.

How shrill the butcher's cat-calls ring,
How loud the lackeys swear!
Black pipe-bowls on the stage they fling,
At Brécourt, fuming there!
The Porter 's stabbed! a Mousquetaire
Breaks in with noisy crew —
'T was all a commonplace affair
When these Old Plays were new!

LA VILLE.

When these Old Plays were new! They bring
A host of phantoms rare:
Old jests that float, old jibes that sting,
Old faces peaked with care:
Ménage's smirk, de Visé's stare,
The thefts of Jean Ribou,—*
Ah, publishers were hard to bear
When these Old Plays were new.

ENVOY.

Ghosts, at your Poet's word ye dare
To break Death's dungeons through,
And frisk, as in that golden air,
When these Old Plays were new!

* A knavish publisher.

BALLADE OF ROULETTE.

TO R. R.

THIS life—one was thinking to-day,
  In the midst of a medley of fancies—
Is a game, and the board where we play
Green earth with her poppies and pansies.
Let *manque* be faded romances,
Be *passé* remorse and regret;
Hearts dance with the wheel as it dances—
The wheel of Dame Fortune's roulette.

The lover will stake as he may
His heart on his Peggies and Nancies;
The girl has her beauty to lay;
The saint has his prayers and his trances;
The poet bets endless expanses
In Dreamland; the scamp has his debt:
How they gaze at the wheel as it glances—
The wheel of Dame Fortune's roulette!

The Kaiser will stake his array
Of sabres, of Krupps, and of lances;
An Englishman punts with his pay,
And glory the *jeton* of France is;
Your artists, or Whistlers or Vances,
Have voices or colours to bet;
Will you moan that its motion askance is—
The wheel of Dame Fortune's roulette?

ENVOY.

The prize that the pleasure enhances?
The prize is—at last to forget
The changes, the chops, and the chances—
The wheel of Dame Fortune's roulette.

BALLADE OF FRÈRE LUBIN.

(Clement Marot's Frère Lubin, though translated by Longfellow and others, has not hitherto been rendered into the original measure, of *ballade à double refrain.*)

SOME ten or twenty times a day,
 To bustle to the town with speed,
To dabble in what dirt he may,—
Le Frère Lubin 's the man you need!
But any sober life to lead
Upon an exemplary plan,
Requires a Christian indeed,—
Le Frère Lubin is *not* the man!

Another's " pile " on his to lay,
With all the craft of guile and greed,
To leave you bare of pence or pay,—
Le Frère Lubin 's the man you need!
But watch him with the closest heed,
And dun him with what force you can,—
He 'll not refund, howe'er you plead,—
Le Frère Lubin is *not* the man!

23

An honest girl to lead astray,
With subtle saw and promised mead,
Requires no cunning crone and grey,—
Le Frère Lubin 's the man you need!
He preaches an ascetic creed,
But,—try him with the water can—
A dog will drink, whate'er his breed,—
Le Frère Lubin is *not* the man!

ENVOY.

In good to fail, in ill succeed,
Le Frère Lubin 's the man you need!
In honest works to lead the van,
Le Frère Lubin is *not* the man!

BALLADE OF QUEEN ANNE.

THE modish Airs,
    The Tansey Brew,
The *Swains* and *Fairs*
In curtained Pew;
Nymphs KNELLER drew,
Books BENTLEY read,—
Who knows them, who?
QUEEN ANNE is dead!

· We buy her Chairs,
Her China blue,
Her red-brick Squares
We build anew;
But ah! we rue,
When all is said,
The tale o'er-true,
QUEEN ANNE is dead!

25

Now *Bulls* and *Bears*,
A ruffling Crew,
With Stocks and Shares,
With Turk and Jew,
Go bubbling through
The Town ill-bred:
The World 's askew,
QUEEN ANNE is dead!

ENVOY.

Friend, praise the new;
The old is fled:
Vivat FROU-FROU!
QUEEN ANNE is dead!

BALLADE OF PRIMITIVE MAN.

TO J. A. FARRER.

HE lived in a cave by the seas,
   He lived upon oysters and foes,
But his list of forbidden degrees,
An extensive morality shows;
Geological evidence goes
To prove he had never a pan,
But he shaved with a shell when he chose,—
'T was the manner of Primitive Man.

He worshipp'd the rain and the breeze,
He worshipp'd the river that flows,
And the Dawn, and the Moon, and the trees,
And bogies, and serpents, and crows;
He buried his dead with their toes
Tucked-up, an original plan,
Till their knees came right under their nose, —
'T was the manner of Primitive Man.

27

His communal wives, at his ease,
He would curb with occasional blows;
Or his State had a queen, like the bees
(As another philosopher trows):
When he spoke, it was never in prose,
But he sang in a strain that would scan,
For (to doubt it, perchance, were morose)
'T was the manner of Primitive Man!

ENVOY.

MAX, proudly your Aryans pose,
But their rigs they undoubtedly ran,
For, as every Darwinian knows,
'T was the manner of Primitive Man!

BALLADE OF SLEEP.

"Of all Gods, Sleep is dearest to the Muses."—Pausanias.

THE hours are passing slow,
    I hear their weary tread
Clang from the tower, and go
Back to their kinsfolk dead.
Sleep! death's twin brother dread!
Why dost thou scorn me so?
The wind's voice overhead
Long wakeful here I know,
And music from the steep
Where waters fall and flow.
Wilt thou not hear me, Sleep?

All sounds that might bestow
Rest on the fever'd bed,
All slumb'rous sounds and low
Are mingled here and wed,
And bring no drowsihed.

Shy dreams flit to and fro
With shadowy hair dispread;
With wistful eyes that glow,
And silent robes that sweep.
Thou wilt not hear me; no?
Wilt thou not hear me, Sleep?

What cause hast thou to show
Of sacrifice unsped?
Of all thy slaves below
I most have labourèd
With service sung and said;
Have cull'd such buds as blow,
Soft poppies white and red,
Where thy still gardens grow,
And Lethe's waters weep.
Why, then, art thou my foe?
Wilt thou not hear me, Sleep?

ENVOY.

Prince, ere the dark be shred
By golden shafts, ere low
And long the shadows creep:
Lord of the wand of lead,
Soft-footed as the snow,
Wilt thou not hear me, Sleep?

BALLADE OF CLEOPATRA'S NEEDLE.

YE giant shades of RA and TUM,
    Ye ghosts of gods Egyptian,
If murmurs of our planet come
To exiles in the precincts wan
Where, fetish or Olympian,
To help or harm no more ye list,
Look down, if look ye may, and scan
This monument in London mist!

Behold, the hieroglyphs are dumb
That once were read of him that ran
When seistron, cymbal, trump, and drum
Wild music of the Bull began;
When through the chanting priestly clan
Walk'd Ramses, and the high sun kiss'd
This stone, with blessing scored and ban —
This monument in London mist.

The stone endures though gods be numb;
Though human effort, plot, and plan
Be sifted, drifted, like the sum
Of sands in wastes Arabian.
What king may deem him more than man,
What priest says Faith can Time resist
While *this* endures to mark their span—
This monument in London mist?

ENVOY.

Prince, the stone's shade on your divan
Falls; it is longer than ye wist:
It preaches, as Time's gnomon can,
This monument in London mist!

BALLADE OF TRUE WISDOM.

WHILE others are asking for beauty or fame,
  Or praying to know that for which they should
    pray,
Or courting Queen Venus, that affable dame,
Or chasing the Muses the weary and grey,
The sage has found out a more excellent way—
To Pan and to Pallas his incense he showers,
And his humble petition puts up day by day,
For a house full of books, and a garden of flowers.

Inventors may bow to the God that is lame,
And crave from the fire on his stithy a ray;
Philosophers kneel to the God without name,
Like the people of Athens, agnostics are they;
The hunter a fawn to Diana will slay,
The maiden wild roses will wreathe for the Hours;
But the wise man will ask, ere libation he pay,
For a house full of books, and a garden of flowers.

Oh! grant me a life without pleasure or blame
(As mortals count pleasure who rush through their day
With a speed to which that of the tempest is tame)!
O grant me a house by the beach of a bay,
Where the waves can be surly in winter, and play
With the sea-weed in summer, ye bountiful powers!
And I 'd leave all the hurry, the noise, and the fray,
For a house full of books, and a garden of flowers.

ENVOY.

Gods, grant or withhold it; your "yea" and your "nay"
Are immutable, heedless of outcry of ours:
But life *is* worth living, and here we would stay
For a house full of books, and a garden of flowers.

BALLADE OF THE MUSE.

Quem tu, Melpomene, semel.

THE man whom once, Melpomene,
    Thou look'st on with benignant sight,
Shall never at the Isthmus be
A boxer eminent in fight,
Nor fares he foremost in the flight
Of Grecian cars to victory,
Nor goes with Delian laurels dight,
The man thou lov'st, Melpomene!

Not him the Capitol shall see,
As who hath crush'd the threats and might
Of monarchs, march triumphantly;
But Fame shall crown him, in his right
Of all the Roman lyre that smite
The first; so woods of Tivoli
Proclaim him, so her waters bright,
The man thou lov'st, Melpomene!

The sons of queenly Rome count *me*,
Me too, with them whose chants delight,—
The poets' kindly company;
Now broken is the tooth of spite,
But thou, that temperest aright
The golden lyre, all, all to thee
He owes—life, fame, and fortune's height—
The man thou lov'st, Melpomene!

ENVOY.

Queen, that to mute lips could'st unite
The wild swan's dying melody!
Thy gifts, ah! how shall he requite—
The man thou lov'st, Melpomene?

BALLADE FOR A BABY.

(FROM "THE GARLAND OF RACHEL.")

'TIS distance lends, the poet says,
    Enchantment to the view,
And this makes possible the praise
Which I bestow on you.
For babies rosy-pink of hue
I do not *always* care,
But distance paints the mountains blue,
And Rachel always fair.

Ah Time, speed on her flying days,
Bring back my youth that flew,
That she may listen to my lays
Where Merton stock-doves coo;
That I may sing afresh, anew,
My songs, now faint and rare,
Time, make me always twenty-two,
And Rachel always fair.

Nay, long ago, down dusky ways
Fled Cupid and his crew;
Life brings not back the morning haze,
The dawning and the dew;
And other lips must sigh and sue,
And younger lovers dare
To hint that Love is always true,
And Rachel always fair.

ENVOY.

Princess, let Age bid Youth adieu,
Adieu to this despair,
To me, who thus despairing woo,
And Rachel always fair.

BALLADE OF HIS OWN COUNTRY.

> I scribbled on a fly-book's leaves
>   Among the shining salmon-flies ;
> A song for summer-time that grieves
>   I scribbled on a fly-book's leaves.
>   Between grey sea and golden sheaves,
> Beneath the soft wet Morvern skies,
> I scribbled on a fly-book's leaves
>   Among the shining salmon-flies.

TO C. H. ARKCOLL.

LET them boast of Arabia, oppressed
    By the odour of myrrh on the breeze ;
In the isles of the East and the West
    That are sweet with the cinnamon trees
Let the sandal-wood perfume the seas ;
    Give the roses to Rhodes and to Crete,
We are more than content, if you please,
    With the smell of bog-myrtle and peat !

Though Dan Virgil enjoyed himself best
  With the scent of the limes, when the bees
Hummed low 'round the doves in their nest,
  While the vintagers lay at their ease,
Had he sung in our northern degrees,
  He 'd have sought a securer retreat,
He 'd have dwelt, where the heart of us flees,
  With the smell of bog-myrtle and peat!

Oh, the broom has a chivalrous crest
  And the daffodil 's fair on the leas,
And the soul of the Southron might rest,
  And be perfectly happy with these;
But *we*, that were nursed on the knees
  Of the hills of the North, we would fleet
Where our hearts might their longing appease
  With the smell of bog-myrtle and peat!

ENVOY.

Princess, the domain of our quest
  It is far from the sounds of the street,
Where the Kingdom of Galloway 's blest
  With the smell of bog-myrtle and peat!

BALLADE OF THE TWEED.

(LOWLAND SCOTCH.)

TO T. W. LANG.

THE ferox rins in rough Loch Awe,
    A weary cry frae ony toun;
The Spey, that loups o'er linn and fa',
They praise a' ither streams aboon;
They boast their braes o' bonny Doon:
Gie *me* to hear the ringing reel,
Where shilfas sing, and cushats croon
By fair Tweed-side, at Ashiesteel!

There 's Ettrick, Meggat, Ail, and a',
Where trout swim thick in May and June;
Ye 'll see them take in showers o' snaw
Some blinking, cauldrife April noon:
Rax ower the palmer and march-broun,
And syne we 'll show a bonny creel,
In spring or simmer, late or soon,
By fair Tweed-side, at Ashiesteel!

There 's mony a water, great or sma',
Gaes singing in his siller tune,
Through glen and heugh, and hope and shaw,
Beneath the sun-licht or the moon:
But set us in our fishing-shoon
Between the Caddon-burn and Peel,
And syne we 'll cross the heather broun
By fair Tweed-side at Ashiesteel!

ENVOY.

Deil take the dirty, trading loon
Wad gar the water ca' his wheel,
And drift his dyes and poisons doun
By fair Tweed-side at Ashiesteel!

BALLADE OF THE ROYAL GAME
OF GOLF.

TO LESLIE BALFOUR.

(East Fifeshire.)

THERE are laddies will drive ye a ba'
    To the burn frae the farthermost tee,
But ye mauna think driving is a',
Ye may heel her, and send her ajee,
Ye may land in the sand or the sea ;
And ye 're dune, sir, ye 're no worth a preen,
Tak' the word that an auld man 'll gie,
Tak' aye tent to be up on the green !

The auld folk are crouse, and they craw
That their putting is pawky and slee ;
In a bunker they 're nae gude ava',
But to girn, and to gar the sand flee.

And a lassie can putt—ony she,—
Be she Maggy, or Bessie, or Jean,
But a cleek-shot 's the billy for me,
Tak' aye tent to be up on the green!

I hae play'd in the frost and the thaw,
I hae play'd since the year thirty-three,
I hae play'd in the rain and the snaw,
And I trust I may play till I dee;
And I tell ye the truth and nae lee,
For I speak o' the thing I hae seen —
Tom Morris, I ken, will agree —
Tak' aye tent to be up on the green!

ENVOY.

Prince, faith you 're improving a wee,
And, Lord, man, they tell me you 're keen;
Tak' the best o' advice that can be,
Tak' aye tent to be up on the green!

BALLADE OF THE MIDNIGHT FOREST.

AFTER THÉODORE DE BANVILLE.

STILL sing the mocking fairies, as of old,
　　Beneath the shade of thorn and holly-tree;
The west wind breathes upon them, pure and cold,
And wolves still dread Diana roaming free
In secret woodland with her company.
'T is thought the peasants' hovels know her rite
When now the wolds are bathed in silver light,
And first the moonrise breaks the dusky grey,
Then down the dells, with blown soft hair and bright,
And through the dim wood Dian threads her way.

With water-weeds twined in their locks of gold,
The strange cold forest-fairies dance in glee;
Sylphs over-timorous and over-bold
Haunt the dark hollows where the dwarf may be,
The wild red dwarf, the nixies' enemy;

Then 'mid their mirth, and laughter, and affright,
The sudden Goddess enters, tall and white,
With one long sigh for summers pass'd away;
The swift feet tear the ivy nets outright,
And through the dim wood Dian threads her way.

She gleans her silvan trophies; down the wold
She hears the sobbing of the stags that flee
Mixed with the music of the hunting roll'd,
But her delight is all in archery,
And naught of ruth and pity wotteth she
More than her hounds that follow on the flight;
The Goddess draws a golden bow of might
And thick she rains the gentle shafts that slay.
She tosses loose her locks upon the night,
And through the dim wood Dian threads her way.

ENVOY.

Prince, let us leave the din, the dust, the spite,
The gloom and glare of towns, the plague, the blight:
Amid the forest leaves and fountain spray
There is the mystic home of our delight,
And through the dim wood Dian threads her way.

BALLADE OF CRICKET.

TO T. W. LANG.

THE burden of hard hitting: slog away!
Here shalt thou score a "five" and there a "four,"
And then upon thy bat shalt lean, and say,
That thou art in for an uncommon score.
Yea, the loud ring applauding thee shall roar,
And thou to rival THORNTON shalt aspire,
When lo, the Umpire gives thee "leg before,"—
"This is the end of every man's desire!"

The burden of much bowling, when the stay
Of all thy team is "collared," swift or slower,
When "bailers" break not in their wonted way,
And "Yorkers" come not off as here-to-fore,
When length balls shoot no more, ah never more,
When all deliveries lose their former fire,
When bats seem broader than the broad barn-door,—
"This is the end of every man's desire!"

47

The burden of long fielding, when the clay
Clings to thy shoon in sudden shower's downpour,
And running still thou stumblest, or the ray
Of blazing suns doth bite and burn thee sore,
And blind thee till, forgetful of thy lore,
Thou dost most mournfully misjudge a "skyer,"
And lose a match the Fates cannot restore,—
"This is the end of every man's desire!"

ENVOY.

Alas, yet liefer on Life's hither shore
Would I be some poor Player on scant hire,
Than King among the old, who play no more,—
"*This* is the end of every man's desire!"

BALLADE OF THE BOOK-MAN'S PARADISE.

THERE *is* a Heaven, or here, or there,—
   A Heaven there is, for me and you,
Where bargains meet for purses spare,
Like ours, are not so far and few.
Thuanus' bees go humming through
The learned groves, 'neath rainless skies,
O'er volumes old and volumes new,
Within that Book-man's Paradise!

There treasures bound for Longepierre
Keep brilliant their morocco blue,
There Hookes' *Amanda* is not rare,
Nor early tracts upon Peru!
Racine is common as Rotrou,
No Shakespeare Quarto search defies,
And Caxtons grow as blossoms grew,
Within that Book-man's Paradise!

There 's Eve,—not our first mother fair,—
But Clovis Eve, a binder true;
Thither does Bauzonnet repair,
Derome, Le Gascon, Padeloup!
But never come the cropping crew
That dock a volume's honest size,
Nor they that "letter" backs askew,
Within that Book-man's Paradise!

ENVOY.

Friend, do not Heber and De Thou,
And Scott, and Southey, kind and wise,
La chasse au bouquin still pursue
Within that Book-man's Paradise?

BALLADE OF WORLDLY WEALTH.

(OLD FRENCH.)

MONEY taketh town and wall,
   Fort and ramp without a blow;
Money moves the merchants all,
While the tides shall ebb and flow;
Money maketh Evil show
Like the Good, and Truth like lies:
These alone can ne'er bestow
Youth, and health, and Paradise.

Money maketh festival,
Wine she buys, and beds can strow;
Round the necks of captains tall,
Money wins them chains to throw,
Marches soldiers to and fro,
Gaineth ladies with sweet eyes:
These alone can ne'er bestow
Youth, and health, and Paradise.

51

Money wins the priest his stall;
Money mitres buys, I trow,
Red hats for the Cardinal,
Abbeys for the novice low;
Money maketh sin as snow,
Place of penitence supplies:
These alone can ne'er bestow
Youth, and health, and Paradise.

BALLADE OF THE MAY TERM.

(Being a Petition, in the form of a Ballade, praying the University Commissioners to spare the Summer Term.)

WHEN Lent and Responsions are ended,
    When May with fritillaries waits,
When the flower of the chestnut is splendid,
When drags are at all of the gates
(Those drags the philosopher "slates"
With a scorn that is truly sublime),*
Life wins from the grasp of the Fates
Sweet hours and the fleetest of time!

When wickets are bowl'd and defended,
When Isis is glad with "the Eights,"
When music and sunset are blended,
When youth and the summer are mates,
When Freshmen are heedless of "Greats,"
And when note-books are cover'd with rhyme,
Ah, these are the hours that one rates —
Sweet hours and the fleetest of time!

   * Cf. "Suggestions for Academic Reorganization."

When the brow of the Dean is unbended
At luncheons and mild tête-à-têtes,
When the Tutor 's in love, nor offended
By blunders in tenses or dates;
When bouquets are purchased of Bates,
When the bells in their melody chime,
When unheeded the Lecturer prates —
Sweet hours and the fleetest of time!

ENVOY.

Reformers of Schools and of States,
Is mirth so tremendous a crime?
Ah! spare what grim pedantry hates —
Sweet hours and the fleetest of time.

4

BALLADE OF DEAD CITIES.

TO E. W. GOSSE.

THE dust of Carthage and the dust
 Of Babel on the desert wold,
The loves of Corinth, and the lust,
Orchomenos increased with gold;
The town of Jason, over-bold,
And Cherson, smitten in her prime —
What are they but a dream half-told?
Where are the cities of old time?

In towns that were a kingdom's trust,
In dim Atlantic forests' fold,
The marble wasteth to a crust,
The granite crumbles into mould;
O'er these — left nameless from of old —
As over Shinar's brick and slime,
One vast forgetfulness is roll'd —
Where are the cities of old time?

The lapse of ages, and the rust,
The fire, the frost, the waters cold,
Efface the evil and the just;
From Thebes, that Eriphyle sold,
To drown'd Caer-Is, whose sweet bells toll'd
Beneath the wave a dreamy chime
That echo'd from the mountain-hold,—
"Where are the cities of old time?"

ENVOY.

Prince, all thy towns and cities must
Decay as these, till all their crime,
And mirth, and wealth, and toil are thrust
Where are the cities of old time.

BALLADE OF THE VOYAGE TO CYTHERA.

AFTER THEODORE DE BANVILLE.

I KNOW Cythera long is desolate;
   I know the winds have stripp'd the gardens green.
Alas, my friends! beneath the fierce sun's weight
A barren reef lies where Love's flowers have been,
Nor ever lover on that coast is seen!
So be it, but we seek a fabled shore,
To lull our vague desires with mystic lore,
To wander where Love's labyrinths beguile;
There let us land, there dream for evermore:
"It may be we shall touch the happy isle."

The sea may be our sepulchre. If Fate,
If tempests wreak their wrath on us, serene
We watch the bolt of heaven, and scorn the hate
Of angry gods that smite us in their spleen.

Perchance the jealous mists are but the screen
That veils the fairy coast we would explore.
Come, though the sea be vex'd, and breakers roar,
Come, for the air of this old world is vile,
Haste we, and toil, and faint not at the oar;
" It may be we shall touch the happy isle."

Grey serpents trail in temples desecrate
Where Cypris smiled, the golden maid, the queen,
And ruined is the palace of our state;
But happy Loves flit round the mast, and keen
The shrill wind sings the silken cords between.
Heroes are we, with wearied hearts and sore,
Whose flower is faded and whose locks are hoar,
Yet haste, light skiffs, where myrtle thickets smile;
Love's panthers sleep 'mid roses, as of yore:
" It may be we shall touch the happy isle !"

ENVOY.

Sad eyes ! the blue sea laughs, as heretofore.
Ah, singing birds your happy music pour !
Ah, poets, leave the sordid earth awhile;
Flit to these ancient gods we still adore:
" It may be we shall touch the happy isle !"

BALLADE OF LIFE.

" ' Dead and gone,'—a sorry burden of the Ballad of Life."
Death's Jest Book.

SAY, fair maids, maying
    In gardens green,
In deep dells straying,
What end hath been
Two Mays between
Of the flowers that shone
And your own sweet queen—
"They are dead and gone!"

Say, grave priests, praying
In dule and teen,
From cells decaying
What have ye seen
Of the proud and mean,
Of Judas and John,
Of the foul and clean?—
"They are dead and gone!"

59

Say, kings, arraying
Loud wars to win,
Of your manslaying
What gain ye glean?
" They are fierce and keen,
But they fall anon,
On the sword that lean,--
They are dead and gone!"

ENVOY.

Through the mad world's scene,
We are drifting on,
To this tune, I ween,
" They are dead and gone!"

BALLADE OF ÆSTHETIC ADJECTIVES.

THERE be "subtle" and "sweet," that are bad
    ones to beat,
There are "lives unlovely," and "souls astray";
There is much to be done yet with "moody" and "meet,"
And "ghastly," and "grimly," and "gaunt," and "grey";
We should ever be "blithesome," but never be gay,
And "splendid" is suited to "summer" and "sea";
"Consummate," they say, is enjoying its day,—
"Intense" is the adjective dearest to me!

The Snows and the Rose they are "windy" and "fleet,"
And "frantic" and "faint" are Delight and Dismay;
Yea, "sanguine," it seems, as the juice of the beet,
Are "the hands of the King" in a general way:
There be loves that quicken, and sicken, and slay;
"Supreme" is the song of the Bard of the free;
But of adjectives all that I name in my lay,
"Intense" is the adjective dearest to me!

61

The Matron intense—let us sit at her feet,
And pelt her with lilies as long as we may;
The Maiden intense—is not always discreet;
But the Singer intense, in his "singing array,"
Will win all the world with his roundelay:
While "blithe" birds carol from tree to tree,
And Art unto Nature doth simper, and say,—
"'Intense' is the adjective dearest to me!"

ENVOY.

Prince, it is surely as good as a play
To mark how the poets and painters agree;
But of plumage æsthetic that feathers the jay,
"Intense" is the adjective dearest to me!

BALLADE OF DEAD LADIES.

AFTER VILLON.

NAY, tell me now in what strange air
    The Roman Flora dwells to-day.
Where Archippiada hides, and where
Beautiful Thais has passed away?
Whence answers Echo, afield, astray,
By mere or stream,—around, below?
Lovelier she than a woman of clay;
Nay, but where is the last year's snow?

Where is wise Héloïse, that care
Brought on Abeilard, and dismay?
All for her love he found a snare,
A maimed poor monk in orders grey;
And where 's the Queen who willed to slay
Buridan, that in a sack must go
Afloat down Seine,—a perilous way—
Nay, but where is the last year's snow?

Where 's that White Queen, a lily rare,
With her sweet song, the Siren's lay?
Where 's Bertha Broad-foot, Beatrice fair?
Alys and Ermengarde, where are they?
Good Joan, whom English did betray
In Rouen town, and burned her? No,
Maiden and Queen, no man may say;
Nay, but where is the last year's snow?

ENVOY.

Prince, all this week thou need'st not pray,
Nor yet this year the thing to know.
One burden answers, ever and aye,
" Nay, but where is the last year's snow?"

VILLON'S BALLADE.

OF GOOD COUNSEL, TO HIS FRIENDS OF EVIL LIFE.

NAY, be you pardoner or cheat,
  Or cogger keen, or mumper shy,
You 'll burn your fingers at the feat,
And howl like other folks that fry.
All evil folks that love a lie!
And where goes gain that greed amasses,
By wile, and guile, and thievery?
'T is all to taverns and to lasses!

Rhyme, rail, dance, play the cymbals sweet,
With game, and shame, and jollity,
Go jigging through the field and street,
With *myst'ry* and *morality;*
Win gold at *gleek,*—and that will fly,
Where all you gain at *passage* passes,—
And that 's? You know as well as I,
'T is all to taverns and to lasses!

65

Nay, forth from all such filth retreat,
Go delve and ditch, in wet or dry,
Turn groom, give horse and mule their meat,
If you 've no clerkly skill to ply;
You 'll gain enough, with husbandry.
But—sow hempseed and such wild grasses,
And where goes all you take thereby?—
'T is all to taverns and to lasses!

ENVOY.

Your clothes, your hose, your broidery,
Your linen that the snow surpasses,
Or ere they 're worn, off, off they fly,
'T is all to taverns and to lasses!

BALLADE AMOUREUSE.

AFTER FROISSART.

NOT Jason nor Medea wise,
  I crave to see, nor win much lore,
Nor list to Orpheus' minstrelsies;
Nor Her'cles would I see, that o'er
The wide world roamed from shore to shore;
Nor, by St. James, Penelope,—
Nor pure Lucrece, such wrong that bore:
To see my Love suffices me!

Virgil and Cato, no man vies
With them in wealth of clerkly store;
I would not see them with mine eyes;
Nor him that sailed, *sans* sail nor oar,
Across the barren sea and hoar,
And all for love of his ladye;
Nor pearl nor sapphire takes me more:
To see my Love suffices me!

I heed not Pegasus, that flies
As swift as shafts the 'bowmen pour;
Nor famed Pygmalion's artifice,
Whereof the like was ne'er before;
Nor Oléus, that drank of yore
The salt wave of the whole great sea:
Why? dost thou ask? 'T is as I swore —
To see my Love suffices me!

BALLADE AGAINST THE JESUITS.

AFTER LA FONTAINE.

ROME does right well to censure all the vain
　　Talk of Jansenius, and of them who preach
That earthly joys are damnable! 'T is plain
We need not charge at Heaven as at a breach;
No, amble on! We 'll gain it, one and all;
The narrow path 's a dream fantastical,
And Arnauld 's quite superfluously driven
Mirth from the world. We 'll scale the heavenly wall,
Escobar makes a primrose path to heaven!

He does not hold a man may well be slain
Who vexes with unseasonable speech,
You *may* do murder for five ducats gain,
Not for a pin, a ribbon, or a peach;
He ventures (most consistently) to teach

That there are certain cases which befall
When perjury need no good man appal,
And life of love (he says) may keep a leaven.
Sure, hearing this, a grateful world will bawl,
" Escobar makes a primrose path to heaven ! "

" For God's sake read me somewhat in the strain
Of his most cheering volumes, I beseech ! "
Why should I name them all? a mighty train —
So many, none may know the name of each.
Make these your compass to the heavenly beach,
These only in your library instal :
Burn Pascal and his fellows, great and small,
Dolts that in vain with Escobar have striven ;
I tell you, and the common voice doth call,
Escobar makes a primrose path to heaven !

ENVOY.

SATAN, that pride did hurry to thy fall,
Thou porter of the grim infernal hall —
Thou keeper of the courts of souls unshriven !
To shun thy shafts, to 'scape thy hellish thrall,
Escobar makes a primrose path to heaven !

BALLADE OF BLIND LOVE.

WHO have loved and ceased to love, forget
    That ever they loved in their lives, they say;
Only remember the fever and fret,
And the pain of Love, that was all his pay;
All the delight of him passes away
From hearts that hoped, and from lips that met—
Too late did I love you, my love, and yet
I shall never forget till my dying day.

Too late were we 'ware of the secret net
That meshes the feet in the flowers that stray;
There were we taken and snared, Lisette,
In the dungeon of La Fausse Amistie;
Help was there none in the wide world's fray,
Joy was there none in the gift and the debt;
Too late we knew it, too long regret —
I shall never forget till my dying day!

We must live our lives, though the sun be set,
Must meet in the masque where parts we play,
Must cross in the maze of Life's minuet;
Our yea is yea, and our nay is nay:
But while snows of winter or flowers of May
Are the sad year's shroud or coronet,
In the season of rose or of violet,
I shall never forget till my dying day!

ENVOY.

Queen, when the clay is my coverlet,
When I am dead, and when you are grey,
Vow, where the grass of the grave is wet,
"I shall never forget till my dying day!"

BALLADE OF HIS CHOICE OF A SEPULCHRE.

HERE I 'd come when weariest!
    Here the breast
Of the Windburg's * tufted over
Deep with bracken ; here his crest
    Takes the west,
Where the wide-winged hawk doth hover.

Silent here are lark and plover ;
    In the cover
Deep below the cushat best
Loves his mate, and croons above her
    O'er their nest,
Where the wide-winged hawk doth hover.

* A hill on the Teviot in Roxburghshire.

Bring me here, Life's tired-out guest,
  To the blest
Bed that waits the weary rover,
Here should failure be confessed;
  Ends my quest,
Where the wide-winged hawk doth hover!

ENVOY.

Friend, or stranger kind, or lover,
Ah, fulfil a last behest,
  Let me rest
Where the wide-winged hawk doth hover!

GRACE À LA MUSE, ET JE LUI DIS MERCI,
J'AI COMPOSÉ MES TRENTE SIX BALLADES!

DIZAIN.

*A*S, *to the pipe, with rhythmic feet*
   In windings of some old-world dance,
The smiling couples cross and meet,
Join hands, and then in line advance,
So, to these fair old tunes of France,
Through all their maze of to-and-fro,
The light-heeled numbers laughing go,
Retreat, return, and ere they flee,
One moment pause in panting row,
And seem to say,—VOS PLAUDITE.

AUSTIN DOBSON.

VERSES VAIN.

77

ALMAE MATRES.

(St. Andrews, 1862.   Oxford, 1865.)

ST. *Andrews by the Northern sea,*
  A haunted town it is to me!
A little city, worn and grey,
  The grey North Ocean girds it round.
And o'er the rocks, and up the bay,
  The long sea-rollers surge and sound.
And still the thin and biting spray
  Drives down the melancholy street,
And still endure, and still decay,
  Towers that the salt winds vainly beat.
Ghost-like and shadowy they stand
Clear mirrored in the wet sea-sand.

O, ruined chapel, long ago
  We loitered idly where the tall
Fresh budded mountain ashes blow
  Within thy desecrated wall:

The tough roots broke the tomb below,
  The April birds sang clamorous,
We did not dream, we could not know
  How soon the Fates would sunder us!

O, broken minster, looking forth
  Beyond the bay, above the town,
O, winter of the kindly North,
  O, college of the scarlet gown,
And shining sands beside the sea,
  And stretch of links beyond the sand,
Once more I watch you, and to me
  It is as if I touched his hand!

And therefore art thou yet more dear,
  O, little city, grey and sere,
Though shrunken from thine ancient pride
  And lonely by thy lonely sea,
Than these fair halls on Isis' side,
  Where Youth an hour came back to me!

A land of waters green and clear,
  Of willows and of poplars tall,
And, in the spring time of the year,
  The white may breaking over all,

And Pleasure quick to come at call.
　And summer rides by marsh and wold,
And Autumn with her crimson pall
　About the towers of Magdalen* rolled;
And strange enchantments from the past,
　And memories of the friends of old,
And strong Tradition, binding fast
　The "flying terms" with bands of gold,—

All these hath Oxford : all are dear,
　But dearer far the little town,
The drifting surf, the wintry year,
　The college of the scarlet gown,
　　St. Andrews by the Northern sea,
　　That is a haunted town to me!

* Pronounced "Maudlin."

NIGHTINGALE WEATHER.

'Serai-je nonnette, oui ou non ?
Serai-je nonnette ? je crois que non.
Derrière chez mon père
Il est un bois taillis,
Le rossignol y chante
Et le jour et la nuit.
Il chante pour les filles
Qui n'ont pas d'ami ;
Il ne chante pas pour moi,
J'en ai un, Dieu merci.'—OLD FRENCH.

I 'LL never be a nun, I trow,
  While apple bloom is white as snow.
But far more fair to see ;
I 'll never wear nun's black and white
While nightingales make sweet the night
  Within the apple tree.

Ah, listen ! 'tis the nightingale,
And in the wood he makes his wail,
  Within the apple tree ;
He singeth of the sore distress
Of many ladies loverless ;
  Thank God, no song for me.

For when the broad May moon is low,
A gold fruit seen where blossoms blow
  In the boughs of the apple tree,
A step I know is at the gate;
Ah love, but it is long to wait
  Until night's noon bring thee!

Between lark's song and nightingale's
A silent space, while dawning pales,
  The birds leave still and free
For words and kisses musical,
For silence and for sighs that fall
  In the dawn, 'twixt him and me.

COLINETTE.

FOR A SKETCH BY MR. G. LESLIE, A.R.A.

FRANCE your country, as we know;
   Room enough for guessing yet,
What lips now or long ago,
   Kissed and named you—Colinette.
In what fields from sea to sea,
   By what stream your home was set,
Loire or Seine was glad of thee,
   Marne or Rhone, O Colinette?

Did you stand with "maidens ten,
   Fairer maids were never seen,"
When the young king and his men
   Passed among the orchards green?
Nay, old ballads have a note
   Mournful, we would fain forget;
No such sad old air should float
   Round your young brows, Colinette.

84

Say, did Ronsard sing to you,
   Shepherdess, to lull his pain,
When the court went wandering through
   Rose pleasances of Touraine?
Ronsard and his famous Rose
   Long are dust the breezes fret;
You, within the garden close,
   You are blooming, Colinette.

Have I seen you proud and gay,
   With a patched and perfumed beau,
Dancing through the summer day,
   Misty summer of Watteau?
Nay, so sweet a maid as you
   Never walked a minuet
With the splendid courtly crew;
   Nay, forgive me, Colinette.

Not from Greuze's canvasses
   Do you cast a glance, a smile;
You are not as one of these,
   Yours is beauty without guile.
Round your maiden brows and hair
   Maidenhood and Childhood met,
Crown and kiss you, sweet and fair,
   New art's blossom, Colinette.

FROM THE EAST TO THE WEST.

RETURNING from what other seas
    Dost thou renew thy murmuring,
Weak Tide, and hast thou aught of these
    To tell, the shores where float and cling
My love, my hope, my memories?

Say does my lady wake to note
    The gold light into silver die?
Or do thy waves make lullaby,
    While dreams of hers, like angels, float
Through star-sown spaces of the sky?

Ah, would such angels came to me
    That dreams of mine might speak with hers,
Nor wake the slumber of the sea
With words as low as winds that be
    Awake among the gossamers!

A DREAM.

WHY will you haunt my sleep?
 You know it may not be,
The grave is wide and deep,
 That sunders you and me;
In bitter dreams we reap
 The sorrow we have sown,
And I would I were asleep,
 Forgotten and alone!

We knew and did not know,
 We saw and did not see,
The nets that long ago
 Fate wove for you and me;
The cruel nets that keep
 The birds that sob and moan,
And I would we were asleep,
 Forgotten and alone!

* * * * * *

TWILIGHT ON TWEED.

THREE crests against the saffron sky,
    Beyond the purple plain,
The dear remembered melody
    Of Tweed once more again.

Wan water from the border hills,
    Dear voice from the old years,
Thy distant music lulls and stills,
    And moves to quiet tears.

Like a loved ghost thy fabled flood
    Fleets through the dusky land;
Where Scott, come home to die, has stood,
    My feet returning stand.

A mist of memory broods and floats,
    The border waters flow;
The air is full of ballad notes,
    Borne out of long ago.

Old songs that sung themselves to me,
  Sweet through a boy's day dream,
While trout below the blossom'd tree
  Plashed in the golden stream.

*   *   *   *   *   *

Twilight, and Tweed, and Eildon Hill,
  Fair and thrice fair you be;
You tell me that the voice is still
  That should have welcomed me.

                          1870.

A SUNSET OF WATTEAU.

LUI.

THE silk sail fills, the soft winds wake,
  Arise and tempt the seas;
Our ocean is the Palace lake,
Our waves the ripples that we make
  Among the mirrored trees.

ELLE.

Nay, sweet the shore, and sweet the song,
  And dear the languid dream;
The music mingled all day long
With paces of the dancing throng,
  And murmur of the stream.

An hour ago, an hour ago,
  We rested in the shade;
And now, why should we seek to know
What way the wilful waters flow?
  There is no fairer glade.

LUI.

Nay, pleasure flits, and we must sail,
   And seek him everywhere;
Perchance in sunset's golden pale
He listens to the nightingale,
   Amid the perfumed air.

Come, he has fled; you are not you,
   And I no more am I;
Delight is changeful as the hue
Of heaven, that is no longer blue
   In yonder sunset sky.

ELLE.

Nay, if we seek we shall not find,
   If we knock none openeth;
Nay, see, the sunset fades behind
The mountains, and the cold night wind
   Blows from the house of Death.

ROMANCE.

MY Love dwelt in a Northern land.
    A grey tower in a forest green
Was his, and far on either hand
    The long wash of the waves was seen,
And leagues on leagues of yellow sand,
    The woven forest boughs between!

And through the clear faint Northern night
    The sunset slowly died away,
And herds of strange deer, silver-white,
    Stole forth among the branches grey;
About the coming of the light,
    They fled like ghosts before the day!

I know not if the forest green
    Still girdles round that castle grey;
I know not if the boughs between
    The white deer vanish ere the day;
Above my Love the grass is green,
    My heart is colder than the clay!

A SUNSET ON YARROW.

THE wind and the day had lived together,
   They died together, and far away
Spoke farewell in the sultry weather,
Out of the sunset, over the heather,
   The dying wind and the dying day.

Far in the south, the summer levin
   Flushed, a flame in the grey soft air:
We seemed to look on the hills of heaven;
You saw within, but to me 't was given
   To see your face, as an angel's, there.

Never again, ah surely never,
   Shall we wait and watch, where of old we stood,
The low good-night of the hill and the river,
The faint light fade, and the wan stars quiver,
   Twain grown one in the solitude.

A PORTRAIT OF 1783.

Y OUR hair and chin are like the hair
   And chin Burne-Jones's ladies wear;
You were unfashionably fair
     In '83 ;
And sad you were when girls are gay,
You read a book about *Le vrai*
Mérite de l'homme, alone in May.
    What *can* it be,
Le vrai mérite de l'homme ? Not gold,
Not titles that are bought and sold,
Not wit that flashes and is cold,
    But Virtue merely !
Instructed by Jean-Jacques Rousseau
(And Jean-Jacques, surely, ought to know),
You bade the crowd of foplings go,
    You glanced severely,

Dreaming beneath the spreading shade
Of "that vast hat the Graces made"; *
So Rouget sang—while yet he played
    With courtly rhyme,
And hymned great Doisi's red perruque,
And Nice's eyes, and Zulmé's look,
And dead canaries, ere he shook
    The sultry time
With strains like thunder. Loud and low
Methinks I hear the murmur grow,
The tramp of men that come and go
    With fire and sword.
They war against the quick and dead,
Their flying feet are dashed with red,
As theirs the vintaging that tread
    Before the Lord.
O head unfashionably fair,
What end was thine, for all thy care?
We only see thee dreaming there:
    We cannot see

    * Vous y verrez, belle Julie,
      Que ce chapeau tout maltraité
      Fut, dans un instant de folie,
      Par les Grâces même inventé.

"À Julie." *Essais en Prose et en Vers*, par Joseph
    Lisle; Paris, An. V. de la République.

The breaking of thy vision, when
The Rights of Man were lords of men,
When virtue won her own again
    In '93.

THE BARBAROUS BIRD-GODS:
A SAVAGE PARABASIS.

[THE myth in the " Birds " of Aristophanes, which represents Birds as older than the Gods, may have been a genuine Greek tradition. The following lines show how prevalent is the myth among widely severed races. The Mexican Bird-gods I omit; who can rhyme to Huitzilopochtli?]

The Birds Sing:

WE would have you to wit, that on eggs though we sit, and are spiked on the spit, and are baked in the pan,
Birds are older by far than your ancestors are, and made love and made war ere the making of Man!
For when all things were dark, not a glimmer nor spark, and the world like a barque without rudder or sail
Floated on through the night, 't was a Bird struck a light, 't was a flash from the bright feather'd Tonatiu's* tail!

* Tonatiu, the Thunder Bird; well known to the Dacotahs and Zulus.

Then the Hawk* with some dry wood flew up in the
    sky, and afar, safe and high, the Hawk lit Sun and
    Moon,
And the Birds of the air they rejoiced everywhere, and
    they recked not of care that should come on them
    soon.
For the Hawk, so they tell, was then known as Pundjel,†
    and a-musing he fell at the close of the day;
Then he went on the quest, as we thought, of a nest,
    with some bark of the best, and a clawful of clay.‡
And with these did he frame two birds lacking a name,
    without feathers (his game was a puzzle to all);
Next around them he fluttered a-dancing, and muttered;
    and, lastly, he uttered a magical call:
Then the figures of clay, as they featherless lay, they
    leaped up, who but they, and embracing they fell,
And *this* was the baking of Man, and his making; but
    now he's forsaking his Father, Pundjel!
Now these creatures of mire, they kept whining for fire,
    and to crown their desire who was found but the
    Wren?

---

  *The Hawk, in the myth of the Galinameros of Central Califor-
nia, lit up the Sun.
  †Pundjel, the Eagle Hawk, is the demiurge and "culture-hero"
of several Australian tribes.
  ‡The Creation of Man is thus described by the Australians.

To the high heaven he came, from the Sun stole he
    flame, and for this has a name in the memory of
    men ! *

And in India who for the Soma juice flew, and to men
    brought it through without falter or fail ?

Why the Hawk 't was again, and great Indra to men
    would appear, now and then, in the shape of a Quail,

While the Thlinkeet's delight is the Bird of the Night,
    the beak and the bright ebon plumage of Yehl. †

And who for man's need brought the famed Suttung's
    mead ? why 't is told in the creed of the Sagamen
    strong,

'T was the Eagle god who brought the drink from the
    blue, and gave mortals the brew that 's the fountain
    of song. ‡

Next, who gave men their laws ? and what reason or
    cause the young brave overawes when in need of a
    squaw,

Till he thinks it a shame to wed one of his name, and
    his conduct you blame if he thus breaks the law ?

---

* In Andaman, Thlinkeet, Melanesian, and other myths, a Bird is
the Prometheus Purphoros ; in Normandy this part is played by the
Wren.

† Yehl : the Raven God of the Thlinkeets.

‡ Indra stole Soma as a Hawk and as a Quail. For Odin's feat
as a Bird, see *Bragi's Telling* in the Younger Edda.

For you still hold it wrong if a *lubra** belong to the
    self-same *kobong* † that is Father of you,
To take *her* as a bride to your ebony side; nay, you
    give her a wide berth; quite right of you, too.
For *her* father, you know, is *your* father, the Crow, and
    no blessing but woe from the wedding would spring.
Well, these rules they were made in the wattle-gum
    shade, and were strictly obeyed, when the Crow was
    the King.‡
Thus on Earth's little ball to the Birds you owe all, yet
    your gratitude's small for the favours they've done,
And their feathers you pill, and you eat them at will,
    yes, you plunder and kill the bright birds one by
    one;
There's a price on their head, and the Dodo is dead,
    and the Moa has fled from the sight of the sun!

*Pundjel, the Eagle Hawk, gave Australians their marriage laws.
†*Lubra*, a woman; *kobong*, "totem"; or, to please Mr. Max
Müller, "otem."
‡The Crow was the Hawk's rival.

POST HOMERICA.

101

HESPEROTHEN.

By the example of certain Grecian mariners, who, being safely returned from the war about Troy, leave yet again their old lands and gods, seeking they know not what, and choosing neither to abide in the fair Phæacian island, nor to dwell and die with the Sirens, at length end miserably in a desert country by the sea, is set forth the *Vanity of Melancholy*. And by the land of Phæacia is to be understood the place of Art and of fair Pleasures; and by Circe's Isle, the places of bodily delights, whereof men, falling aweary attain to Eld, and to the darkness of that age. Which thing Master Fran-çoys Rabelais feigned, under the similitude of the Isle of the Macræones.

THE SEEKERS FOR PHÆACIA.

THERE is a land in the remotest day,
  Where the soft night is born, and sunset dies:
The eastern shores see faint tides fade away,
  That wash the lands where laughter, tears, and sighs,
Make life,—the lands beneath the blue of common skies.

103

But in the west is a mysterious sea,
    (What sails have seen it, or what shipmen known?)
With coasts enchanted where the Sirens be,
    With islands where a Goddess walks alone,
And in the cedar trees the magic winds make moan.

Eastward the human cares of house and home,
    Cities, and ships, and unknown Gods, and loves;
Westward, strange maidens fairer than the foam,
    And lawless lives of men, and haunted groves,
Wherein a God may dwell, and where the Dryad roves.

The Gods are careless of the days and death
    Of toilsome men, beyond the western seas;
The Gods are heedless of their painful breath,
    And love them not, for they are not as these;
But in the golden west they live and lie at ease.

Yet the Phæacians well they love, who live
    At the light's limit, passing careless hours,
Most like the Gods; and they have gifts to give,
    Even wine, and fountains musical, and flowers,
And song, and if they will, swift ships, and magic powers.

It is a quiet midland; in the cool
   Of twilight comes the God, though no man prayed,
To watch the maids and young men beautiful
   Dance, and they see him, and are not afraid,
For they are near of kin to Gods, and undismayed.

Ah, would the bright red prows might bring us nigh
   The dreamy isles that the Immortals keep!
But with a mist they hide them wondrously,
   And far the path and dim to where they sleep,—
The loved, the shadowy lands along the shadowy deep.

THE DEPARTURE FROM PHÆACIA.

THE PHÆACIANS.

WHY from the dreamy meadows,
　　More fair than any dream,
Why will you seek the shadows
　　Beyond the ocean stream?

Through straits of storm and peril,
　　Through firths unsailed before,
Why make you for the sterile,
　　The dark Kimmerian shore?

There no bright streams are flowing,
　　There day and night are one,
No harvest time, no sowing,
　　No sight of any sun;

No sound of song or tabor,
　　No dance shall greet you there;
No noise of mortal labour,
　　Breaks on the blind chill air.

Are ours not happy places,
  Where Gods with mortals trod?
Saw not our sires the faces
  Of many a present God?

THE SEEKERS.

NAY, now no God comes hither,
  In shape that men may see;
They fare we know not whither,
  We know not what they be.

Yea, though the sunset lingers
  Far in your fairy glades,
Though yours the sweetest singers,
  Though yours the kindest maids,

Yet here be the true shadows,
  Here in the doubtful light;
Amid the dreamy meadows
  No shadow haunts the night.

We seek a city splendid,
  With light beyond the sun;
Or lands where dreams are ended,
  And works and days are done.

A BALLAD OF DEPARTURE.*

FAIR white bird, what song art thou singing
    In wintry weather of lands o'er sea?
Dear white bird, what way art thou winging,
    Where no grass grows, and no green tree?

I looked at the far off fields and grey,
    There grew no tree but the cypress tree,
That bears sad fruits with the flowers of May,
    And whoso looks on it, woe is he.

And whoso eats of the fruit thereof
Has no more sorrow, and no more love;
And who sets the same in his garden stead,
In a little space he is waste and dead.

We seek a city splendid,
    With light beyond the sun;
Or lands where dreams are ended,
    And works and days are done.

* From the Romaic.

THEY HEAR THE SIRENS FOR THE SECOND TIME.

THE weary sails a moment slept,
  The oars were silent for a space,
As past Hesperian shores we swept,
  That were as a remembered face
Seen after lapse of hopeless years,
  In Hades, when the shadows meet,
Dim through the mist of many tears,
  And strange, and though a shadow, sweet.

So seemed the half-remembered shore,
  That slumbered, mirrored in the blue,
With havens where we touched of yore,
  And ports that over well we knew.
Then broke the calm before a breeze
  That sought the secret of the west;
And listless all we swept the seas
  Towards the Islands of the Blest.

Beside a golden sanded bay
  We saw the Sirens, very fair
The flowery hill whereon they lay,
  The flowers set upon their hair.
Their old sweet song came down the wind,
  Remembered music waxing strong,
Ah now no need of cords to bind,
  No need had we of Orphic song.

It once had seemed a little thing,
  To lay our lives down at their feet,
That dying we might hear them sing,
  And dying see their faces sweet;
But now, we glanced, and passing by,
  No care had we to tarry long;
Faint hope, and rest, and memory
  Were more than any Siren's song.

CIRCE'S ISLE REVISITED.

AH, Circe, Circe! in the wood we cried;
  Ah, Circe, Circe! but no voice replied;
No voice from bowers o'ergrown and ruinous
As fallen rocks upon the mountain side.

There was no sound of singing in the air;
Faded or fled the maidens that were fair,
  No more for sorrow or joy were seen of us,
No light of laughing eyes, or floating hair.

The perfume, and the music, and the flame
Had passed away; the memory of shame
  Alone abode, and stings of faint desire,
And pulses of vague quiet went and came.

Ah, Circe! in thy sad changed fairy place,
Our dead Youth came and looked on us a space,
  With drooping wings, and eyes of faded fire,
And wasted hair about a weary face.

Why had we ever sought the magic isle
That seemed so happy in the days erewhile?
  Why did we ever leave it, where we met
A world of happy wonders in one smile?

Back to the westward and the waning light
We turned, we fled; the solitude of night
  Was better than the infinite regret,
In fallen places of our dead delight.

THE LIMIT OF LANDS.

BETWEEN the circling ocean sea
  And the poplars of Persephone
There lies a strip of barren sand,
Flecked with the sea's last spray, and strown
With waste leaves of the poplars, blown
  From gardens of the shadow land.

With altars of old sacrifice
The shore is set, in mournful wise
  The mists upon the ocean brood;
Between the water and the air
The clouds are born that float and fare
  Between the water and the wood.

Upon the grey sea never sail
Of mortals passed within our hail,
  Where the last weak waves faint and flow;
We heard within the poplar pale
The murmur of a doubtful wail
  Of voices loved so long ago.

We scarce had care to die or live,
We had no honey cake to give,
   No wine of sacrifice to shed;
There lies no new path over sea,
And now we know how faint they be,
   The feasts and voices of the Dead.

Ah, flowers and dance! ah, sun and snow!
Glad life, sad life we did forego
   To dream of quietness and rest;
Ah, would the fleet sweet roses here
Poured light and perfume through the drear
   Pale year, and wan land of the west.

Sad youth, that let the spring go by
Because the spring is swift to fly,
   Sad youth, that feared to mourn or love,
Behold how sadder far is this,
To know that rest is nowise bliss,
   And darkness is the end thereof.

THE SHADE OF HELEN.

SOME say that Helen went never to Troy, but abode in Egypt; for the Gods,
having made in her semblance a woman out of clouds and shadows, sent the
same to be wife to Paris. For this shadow then the Greeks and Trojans slew
each other.

(Written in the Pyrenees.)

WHY from the quiet hollows of the hills,
    And extreme meeting place of light and shade,
Wherein soft rains fell slowly, and became
Clouds among sister clouds, where fair spent beams
And dying glories of the sun would dwell,
Why have they whom I know not, nor may know,
Strange hands, unseen and ruthless, fashioned me,
And borne me from the silent shadowy hills,
Hither, to noise and glow of alien life,
To harsh and clamorous swords, and sound of war?
One speaks unto me words that would be sweet,
Made harsh, made keen with love that knows me not,
And some strange force, within me or around,

115

Makes answer, kiss for kiss, and sigh for sigh,
And somewhere there is fever in the halls,
That troubles me, for no such trouble came
To vex the cool far hollows of the hills.

The foolish folk crowd round me, and they cry,
That house, and wife, and lands, and all Troy town,
Are little to lose, if they may hold me here,
And see me flit, a pale and silent shade,
Among the streets bereft, and helpless shrines.

At other hours another life seems mine,
Where one great river runs unswollen of rain,
By pyramids of unremembered kings,
And homes of men obedient to the Dead.
There dark and quiet faces come and go
Around me, then again the shriek of arms,
And all the turmoil of the Ilian men.
What are they? even shadows such as I.
What make they? Even this — the sport of Gods —
The sport of Gods, however free they seem.
Ah would the game were ended, and the light,
The blinding light, and all too mighty suns,
Withdrawn, and I once more with sister shades,
Unloved, forgotten, mingled with the mist,
Dwelt in the hollows of the shadowy hills.

PISIDICÊ.

THE incident is from the Love Stories of Parthenius, who preserved fragments of a lost epic on the expedition of Achilles against Lesbos, an island allied with Troy.

THE daughter of the Lesbian king
   Within her bower she watched the war,
Far off she heard the arrows ring,
   The smitten harness ring afar ;
And, fighting from the foremost car,
   Saw one that smote where all must flee ;
More fair than the Immortals are
   He seemed to fair Pisidicê !

She saw, she loved him, and her heart
   Before Achilles, Peleus' son,
Threw all its guarded gates apart,
   A maiden fortress lightly won !
And, ere that day of fight was done,
   No more of land or faith recked she,
But joyed in her new life begun,—
   Her life of love, Pisidicê !

She took a gift into her hand,
   As one that had a boon to crave;
She stole across the ruined land
   Where lay the dead without a grave,
And to Achilles' hand she gave
   Her gift, the secret postern's key.
" To-morrow let me be thy slave ! "
   Moaned to her love Pisidicê.

Ere dawn the Argives' clarion call
   Rang down Methymna's burning street;
They slew the sleeping warriors all,
   They drove the women to the fleet,
Save one, that to Achilles' feet
   Clung, but, in sudden wrath, cried he:
" For her no doom but death is meet."
   And there men stoned Pisidicê.

In havens of that haunted coast,
   Amid the myrtles of the shore,
The moon sees many a maiden ghost,—
   Love's outcast now and evermore.
The silence hears the shades deplore
   Their hour of dear-bought love ; but *thee*
The waves lull, 'neath thine olives hoar,
   To dreamless rest, Pisidicê !

SONNETS.

THE ODYSSEY.

A S one that for a weary space has lain
    Lulled by the song of Circe and her wine
  In gardens near the pale of Proserpine,
Where that Ææan isle forgets the main,
And only the low lutes of love complain,
  And only shadows of wan lovers pine,
  As such an one were glad to know the brine
Salt on his lips, and the large air again,—
So gladly, from the songs of modern speech
  Men turn, and see the stars, and feel the free
  Shrill wind beyond the close of heavy flowers,
  And through the music of the languid hours,
They hear like ocean on a western beach
  The surge and thunder of the Odyssey.

TWO SONNETS OF THE SIRENS.

"Les Sirènes estoient tant intimes amies et fidelles compagnes de Proserpine, qu' elles estoient toujours ensemble. Esmues du juste deuil de la perte de leur chère compagne, et enuyées jusques au desespoir, elles s'arrestèrent à la mer Sicilienne, où par leurs chants elles attiroient les navigans, mais l'unique fin de la volupté de leur musique est la Mort."—*Pontus de Tyard* 1570.

I.

THE Sirens once were maidens innocent
   That through the water-meads with Proserpine
Plucked no fire-hearted flowers, but were content
   Cool fritillaries and flag-flowers to twine,
   With lilies woven and with wet woodbine;
Till forth to seek Ætnæan buds they went,
And their kind lady from their choir was rent
   By Hades, down the irremeable decline.
And they have sought her all the wide world through,
   Till many years, and wisdom, and much wrong,
Have filled and changed their song, and o'er the blue
   Rings deadly sweet the magic of the song,
And whoso hears must listen till he die
Far on the flowery shores of Sicily.

II.

So is it with this singing art of ours,
  That once with maids went, maidenlike, and played
  With woven dances in the poplar-shade,
And all her song was but of lady's bowers
And the returning swallows, and spring-flowers,
  Till forth to seek a shadow-queen she strayed,
  A shadowy land; and now hath overweighed
Her singing chaplet with the snow and showers.
And running rivers for the bitter brine
  She left, and by the margin of life's sea
    Sings, and her song is full of the sea's moan,
And wild with dread, and love of Proserpine;
  And whoso once has listened to her, he
    His whole life long is slave to her alone.

LOVE'S EASTER.

L OVE died here
        Long ago;
O'er his bier,
      Lying low,
      Poppies throw;
        Shed no tear;
        Year by year,
      Roses blow!

Year by year,
Adon — dear
    To Love's Queen —
      Does not die!
      Wakes when green
        May is nigh!

124

TWILIGHT.

SONNET.

(AFTER RICHEPIN.)

L IGHT has flown !
　　Through the grey
　The wind's way
The sea's moan
Sound alone !
　For the day
　These repay
And atone !

Scarce I know,
Listening so
　To the streams
　Of the sea,
If old dreams
　Sing to me !

BION.

THE wail of Moschus on the mountains crying
   The Muses heard, and loved it long ago;
They heard the hollows of the hills replying,
   They heard the weeping water's overflow;
They winged the sacred strain — the song undying,
   The song that all about the world must go, —
When poets for a poet dead are sighing,
   The minstrels for a minstrel friend laid low.

And dirge to dirge that answers, and the weeping
   For Adonais by the summer sea,
The plaints for Lycidas, and Thyrsis (sleeping
   Far from " the forest ground called Thessaly "), —
These hold thy memory, Bion, in their keeping,
   And are but echoes of the moan for thee.

SAN TERENZO.

(The village in the bay of Spezia, near which Shelley was living before the wreck of the Don Juan.)

MID April seemed like some November day,
   When through the glassy waters, dull as lead,
Our boat, like shadowy barques that bear the dead,
   Slipped down the curved shores of the Spezian bay,
   Rounded a point,—and San Terenzo lay
Before us, that gay village, yellow and red,
With walls that covered Shelley's homeless head,—
   His house, a place deserted, bleak and grey.

The waves broke on the door-step; fishermen
   Cast their long nets, and drew, and cast again.
   Deep in the ilex woods we wandered free,
When suddenly the forest glades were stirred
   With waving pinions, and a great sea bird
Flew forth, like Shelley's spirit, to the sea!

127

NATURAL THEOLOGY.

ἐπεὶ καὶ τοῦτον ὀΐομαι ἀθανάτοισιν
εὐχεσθαι· Πάντες δὲ θεῶν χατέουσ' ἄνθρωποι.
OD. III. 47.

" ONCE CAGN was like a father, kind and good,
     But He was spoiled by fighting many things;
He wars upon the lions in the wood,
     And breaks the Thunder-bird's tremendous wings;
But still we cry to Him,—*We are thy brood—*
O Cagn, be merciful! and us He brings
To herds of elands, and great store of food,
     And in the desert opens water-springs."

So Qing, King Nqsha's Bushman hunter, spoke,
     Beside the camp-fire, by the fountain fair,
When all were weary, and soft clouds of smoke
     Were fading, fragrant, in the twilit air:
And suddenly in each man's heart there woke
     A pang, a sacred memory of prayer.

HOMER.

HOMER, thy song men liken to the sea,
    With all the notes of music in its tone,
With tides that wash the dim dominion
Of Hades, and light waves that laugh in glee
Around the isles enchanted ; nay, to me
    Thy verse seems as the River of source unknown
    That glasses Egypt's temples overthrown
In his sky-nurtured stream, eternally.

No wiser we than men of heretofore
    To find thy sacred fountains guarded fast ;
Enough, thy flood makes green our human shore,
    As Nilus Egypt, rolling down his vast
His fertile flood, that murmurs evermore
    Of gods dethroned, and empires in the past.

RONSARD.

MASTER, I see thee with the locks of grey,
   Crowned by the Muses with the laurel-wreath;
   I see the roses hiding underneath,
Cassandra's gift; she was less dear than they.
Thou, Master, first hast roused the lyric lay,
   The sleeping song that the dead years bequeath,
   Hast sung thine answer to the songs that breathe
Through ages, and through ages far away.

And thou hast heard the pulse of Pindar beat,
   Known Horace by the fount Bardusian!
Their deathless line thy living strains repeat,
   But ah, thy voice is sad, thy roses wan,
But ah, thy honey is not cloying sweet,
   Thy bees have fed on yews Sardinian.

GÉRARD DE NERVAL.

OF all that were thy prisons—ah, untamed,
  Ah, light and sacred soul !—none holds thee now;
No wall, no bar, no body of flesh, but thou
Art free and happy in the lands unnamed,
Within whose gates, with weary wings and maimed,
  Thou still would'st bear that mystic golden bough
  The Sibyl doth to singing men allow,
Yet thy report folk heeded not, but blamed.
  And they would smile and wonder, seeing where
Thou stood'st, to watch light leaves, or clouds, or wind,
  Dreamily murmuring a ballad air,
Caught from the Valois peasants; dost thou find
  A new life gladder than the old times were,
A love as fair as Sylvie, and more kind?

IN ITHACA.

"AND now am I greatly repenting that ever I left my life with thee, and the immortality thou didst promise me."—*Letter of Odysseus to Calypso.* Luciani *Vera Historia.*

'TIS thought Odysseus when the strife was o'er
   With all the waves and wars, a weary while,
Grew restless in his disenchanted isle,
And still would watch the sunset, from the shore,
Go down the ways of gold, and evermore
   His sad heart followed after, mile on mile,
   Back to the Goddess of the magic wile,
Calypso, and the love that was of yore.

Thou too, thy haven gained, must turn thee yet
   To look across the sad and stormy space,
   Years of a youth as bitter as the sea,
Ah, with a heavy heart, and eyelids wet,
   Because, within a fair forsaken place
   The life that might have been is lost to thee.

DREAMS.

HE spake not truth, however wise,* who said
   "That happy, and that hapless men in sleep
  Have equal fortune, fallen from care as deep
As countless, careless, races of the dead."
Not so, for alien paths of dreams we tread,
  And one beholds the faces that he sighs
  In vain to bring before his daylit eyes,
And waking, he remembers on his bed;

And one with fainting heart and feeble hand
Fights a dim battle in a doubtful land,
  Where strength and courage were of no avail;
And one is borne on fairy breezes far
To the bright harbours of a golden star
  Down fragrant fleeting waters rosy pale.

* Aristotle.

133

HOMERIC UNITY.

THE sacred keep of Ilion is rent
　　With trench and shaft; foiled waters wander slow
Through plains where Simois and Scamander went
　　To war with Gods and heroes long ago.
　　Not yet to tired Cassandra, lying low
In rich Mycenæ, do the Fates relent:
　　The bones of Agamemnon are a show,
And ruined is his royal monument.

The dust and awful treasures of the Dead,
　　Hath Learning scattered wide, but vainly thee,
Homer, she meteth with her tool of lead,
　　And strives to rend thy songs; too blind to see
The crown that burns on thine immortal head
　　Of indivisible supremacy!

IDEAL.

SUGGESTED by a female head in wax, of unknown date, but supposed to be either
of the best Greek age, or a work of Raphael or Leonardo. It is now in the
Lille Museum.

AH, mystic child of Beauty, nameless maid,
   Dateless and fatherless, how long ago,
A Greek, with some rare sadness overweighed,
   Shaped thee, perchance, and quite forgot his woe !
   Or Raphael thy sweetness did bestow,
While magical his fingers o'er thee strayed,
   Or that great pupil of Verrocchio
Redeemed thy still perfection from the shade

That hides all fair things lost, and things unborn,
   Where one has fled from me, that wore thy grace,
   And that grave tenderness of thine awhile ;
Nay, still in dreams I see her, but her face
   Is pale, is wasted with a touch of scorn,
   And only on thy lips I find her smile.

135

TRANSLATIONS.

HYMN TO THE WINDS.

The winds are invoked by the winnowers of corn.

Du Bellay, 1550.

TO you, troop so fleet,
   That with winged wandering feet
  Through the wide world pass,
And with soft murmuring
Toss the green shades of spring
  In woods and grass,
Lily and violet
I give, and blossoms wet,
  Roses and dew;
This branch of blushing roses,
Whose fresh bud uncloses,
  Wind-flowers too.
Ah, winnow with sweet breath,
Winnow the holt and heath,
  Round this retreat;
Where all the golden morn
We fan the gold o' the corn
  In the sun's heat.

A VOW TO HEAVENLY VENUS.

Du Bellay, 1550.

WE that with like hearts love, we lovers twain,
New wedded in the village by thy fane,
Lady of all chaste love, to thee it is
We bring these amaranths, these white lilies,
A sign, and sacrifice; may Love, we pray,
Like amaranthine flowers, feel no decay;
Like these cool lilies may our loves remain,
Perfect and pure, and know not any stain;
And be our hearts, from this thy holy hour,
Bound each to each, like flower to wedded flower.

APRIL.

Remy Belleau, 1560.

A PRIL, pride of woodland ways,
    Of glad days,
April, bringing hope of prime
    To the young flowers that beneath
    Their bud sheath
Are guarded in their tender time ;

April, pride of fields that be
    Green and free,
That in fashion glad and gay
Stud with flowers red and blue,
    Every hue,
Their jewelled spring array ;

April, pride of murmuring
    Winds of spring,
That beneath the winnowed air
Trap with subtle nets and sweet
    Flora's feet,
Flora's feet, the fleet and fair ;

April, by thy hand caressed,
    From her breast
Nature scatters everywhere
Handfuls of all sweet perfumes,
    Buds and blooms,
Making faint the earth and air.

April, joy of the green hours,
    Clothes with flowers
Over all her locks of gold
My sweet Lady ; and her breast
    With the blest
Buds of summer manifold.

April, with thy gracious wiles,
    Like the smiles,
Smiles of Venus ; and thy breath
Like her breath, the Gods' delight,
    (From their height
They take the happy air beneath ;)

It is thou that, of thy grace,
    From their place
In the far-off isles dost bring
Swallows over earth and sea,
    Glad to be
Messengers of thee, and Spring.

Daffodil and eglantine,
    And woodbine,
Lily, violet, and rose
Plentiful in April fair,
    To the air,
Their pretty petals do unclose.

Nightingales ye now may hear,
    Piercing clear,
Singing in the deepest shade ;
Many and many a babbled note
    Chime and float.
Woodland music through the glade.

April, all to welcome thee,
    Spring sets free
Ancient flames, and with low breath
Wakes the ashes grey and old
    That the cold
Chilled within our hearts to death.

Thou beholdest in the warm
    Hours, the swarm
Of the thievish bees, that flies
Evermore from bloom to bloom
    For perfume,
Hid away in tiny thighs.

Her cool shadows May can boast,
    Fruits almost
Ripe, and gifts of fertile dew,
Manna-sweet and honey-sweet,
    That complete
Her flower garland fresh and new.

Nay, but I will give my praise
    To these days,
Named with the glad name of her *
That from out the foam o' the sea
    Came to be
Sudden light on earth and air.

      * Aphrodite — Avril.

OF HIS LADY'S OLD AGE.

Ronsard, 1550.

WHEN you are very old, at evening
  You 'll sit and spin beside the fire, and say,
Humming my songs, "Ah well, ah well-a-day!
When I was young, of me did Ronsard sing."
None of your maidens that doth hear the thing,
  Albeit with her weary task foredone,
  But wakens at my name, and calls you one
Blest, to be held in long remembering.

I shall be low beneath the earth, and laid
On sleep, a phantom in the myrtle shade,
  While you beside the fire, a grandame grey,
My love, your pride, remember and regret;
Ah, love me, love! we may be happy yet,
  And gather roses, while 't is called to-day.

SHADOWS OF HIS LADY.

Jacques Tahureau, 1527-1555.

WITHIN the sand of what far river lies
  The gold that gleams in tresses of my Love?
 What highest circle of the Heavens above
Is jewelled with such stars as are her eyes?
And where is the rich sea whose coral vies
 With her red lips, that cannot kiss enough?
 What dawn-lit garden knew the rose, whereof
The fled soul lives in her cheeks' rosy guise?

What Parian marble that is loveliest,
Can match the whiteness of her brow and breast?
 When drew she breath from the Sabæan glade?
Oh happy rock and river, sky and sea,
Gardens, and glades Sabæan, all that be
 The far-off splendid semblance of my maid!

MOONLIGHT.

Jacques Tahureau, 1527–1555.

THE high Midnight was garlanding her head
   With many a shining star in shining skies,
And, of her grace, a slumber on mine eyes,
   And, after sorrow, quietness was shed.
Far in dim fields cicalas jargonéd
   A thin shrill clamour of complaints and cries;
   And all the woods were pallid, in strange wise,
With pallor of the sad moon overspread.

Then came my lady to that lonely place,
And, from her palfrey stooping, did embrace
   And hang upon my neck, and kissed me over;
Wherefore the day is far less dear than night,
And sweeter is the shadow than the light,
   Since night has made me such a happy lover.

THE GRAVE AND THE ROSE.

VICTOR HUGO.

THE Grave said to the Rose,
   "What of the dews of dawn,
Love's flower, what end is theirs?"
  "And what of spirits flown,
The souls whereon doth close
  The tomb's mouth unawares?"
The Rose said to the Grave.

The Rose said, "In the shade
  From the dawn's tears is made
A perfume faint and strange,
  Amber and honey sweet."
  "And all the spirits fleet
Do suffer a sky-change,
  More strangely than the dew,
  To God's own angels new,"
The Grave said to the Rose.

THE BIRTH OF BUTTERFLIES.

VICTOR HUGO.

THE dawn is smiling on the dew that covers
The tearful roses; lo, the little lovers
That kiss the buds, and all the flutterings
In jasmine bloom, and privet, of white wings,
That go and come, and fly, and peep and hide,
With muffled music, murmured far and wide !
Ah, Spring time, when we think of all the lays
That dreamy lovers send to dreamy mays,
Of the fond hearts within a billet bound,
Of all the soft silk paper that pens wound,
The messages of love that mortals write
Filled with intoxication of delight,
Written in April, and before the May time
Shredded and flown, play things for the wind's playtime,
We dream that all white butterflies above,
Who seek through clouds or waters souls to love,
And leave their lady mistress in despair,
To flit to flowers, as kinder and more fair,
Are but torn love-letters, that through the skies
Flutter, and float, and change to Butterflies.

AN OLD TUNE.

GERARD DE NERVAL.

THERE is an air for which I would disown
   Mozart's, Rossini's, Weber's melodies,—
A sweet sad air that languishes and sighs,
   And keeps its secret charm for me alone.

Whene'er I hear that music vague and old,
   Two hundred years are mist that rolls away;
The thirteenth Louis reigns, and I behold
   A green land golden in the dying day.

An old red castle, strong with stony towers,
   The windows gay with many coloured glass,
Wide plains, and rivers flowing among flowers,
   That bathe the castle basement as they pass.

In antique weed, with dark eyes and gold hair,
   A lady looks forth from her window high;
It may be that I knew and found her fair,
   In some forgotten life, long time gone by.

SPRING IN THE STUDENT'S QUARTER.

HENRI MURGER.

WINTER is passing, and the bells
    For ever with their silver lay
Murmur a melody that tells
    Of April and of Easter day.
High in the sweet air the light vane sets,
    The weathercocks all southward twirl;
A sou will buy her violets
    And make Nini a happy girl.

The winter to the poor was sore,
    Counting the weary winter days,
Watching his little fire-wood store,
    The bitter snow-flakes fell always;
And now his last log dimly gleamed,
    Lighting the room with feeble glare,
Half cinder and half smoke it seemed
    That the wind wafted into air.

Pilgrims from ocean and far isles
    See where the east is reddening,
The flocks that fly a thousand miles
    From sunsetting to sunsetting;
Look up, look out, behold the swallows,
    The throats that twitter, the wings that beat;
And on their song the summer follows,
    And in the summer life is sweet.

*   *   *   *   *

With the green tender buds that know
    The shoot and sap of lusty spring
My neighbour of a year ago
    Her casement, see, is opening;
Through all the bitter months that were,
    Forth from her nest she dared not flee,
She was a study for Boucher,
    She now might sit to Gavarni.

SPRING.

(After Meleager.)

NOW the bright crocus flames, and now
    The slim narcissus takes the rain,
And, straying o'er the mountain's brow,
    The daffodilies bud again.
The thousand blossoms wax and wane
On wold, and heath, and fragrant bough;
But fairer than the flowers art thou,
    Than any growth of hill or plain.

Ye gardens, cast your leafy crown,
That my Love's feet may tread it down,
    Like lilies on the lilies set;
My Love, whose lips are softer far
Than drowsy poppy petals are,
    And sweeter than the violet!

OLD LOVES.

HENRI MURGER.

LOUISE, have you forgotten yet
   The corner of the flowery land,
The ancient garden where we met,
   My hand that trembled in your hand?
Our lips found words scarce sweet enough,
   As low beneath the willow-trees
We sat; have you forgotten, love?
   Do you remember, love Louise?

Marie, have you forgotten yet
   The loving barter that we made?
The rings we changed, the suns that set,
   The woods fulfilled with sun and shade?
The fountains that were musical
   By many an ancient trysting tree —
Marie, have you forgotten all?
   Do you remember, love Marie?

Christine, do you remember yet
  Your room with scents and roses gay?
My garret — near the sky 't was set —
  The April hours, the nights of May?
The clear calm nights — the stars above
  That whispered they were fairest seen
Through no cloud-veil? Remember, love!
  Do you remember, love Christine?

Louise is dead, and, well-a-day!
  Marie a sadder path has ta'en;
And pale Christine has passed away
  In southern suns to bloom again.
Alas! for one and all of us —
  Marie, Louise, Christine forget;
Our bower of love is ruinous,
  And I alone remember yet.

IANNOULA.

ROMAIC FOLK-SONG.

ALL the maidens were merry and wed
    All to lovers so fair to see;
The lover I took to my bridal bed
    He is not long for love and me.

I spoke to him and he nothing said,
    I gave him bread of the wheat so fine,
He did not eat of the bridal bread,
    He did not drink of the bridal wine.

I made him a bed was soft and deep,
    I made him a bed to sleep with me;
"Look on me once before you sleep,
    And look on the flower of my fair body.

"Flowers of April, and fresh May-dew,
    Dew of April and buds of May;
Two white blossoms that bud for you,
    Buds that blossom before the day."

THE MILK WHITE DOE.

FRENCH VOLKS-LIED.

IT was a mother and a maid
  That walked the woods among,
And still the maid went slow and sad,
  And still the mother sung.

"What ails you, daughter Margaret?
  Why go you pale and wan?
Is it for a cast of bitter love,
  Or for a false leman?"

"It is not for a false lover
  That I go sad to see;
But it is for a weary life
  Beneath the greenwood tree.

"For ever in the good daylight
  A maiden may I go,
But always on the ninth midnight
  I change to a milk white doe.

" They hunt me through the green forest
  With hounds and hunting men ;
And ever it is my fair brother
  That is so fierce and keen."

  * * * *

" Good-morrow, mother." " Good-morrow, son ;
  Where are your hounds so good ? "
" Oh, they are hunting a white doe
  Within the glad greenwood.

" And three times have they hunted her,
  And thrice she 's won away ;
The fourth time that they follow her
  That white doe they shall slay."

  * * * * *

Then out and spoke the forester,
  As he came from the wood,
" Now never saw I maid's gold hair
  Among the wild deer's blood.

" And I have hunted the wild deer
  In east lands and in west ;
And never saw I white doe yet
  That had a maiden's breast."

158

Then up and spake her fair brother,
  Between the wine and bread.
" Behold, I had but one sister,
  And I have been her dead.

' But ye must bury my sweet sister
  With a stone at her foot and her head,
And ye must cover her fair body
  With the white roses and red.

" And I must out to the greenwood,
  The roof shall never shelter me ;
And I shall lie for seven long years
  On the grass below the hawthorn tree."

A LA BELLE HELÈNE.

(After Ronsard.)

MORE closely than the clinging vine
    About the wedded tree,
Clasp thou thine arms, ah, mistress mine !
    About the heart of me.
Or seem to sleep, and stoop your face
    Soft on my sleeping eyes,
Breathe in your life, your heart, your grace,
    Through me, in kissing wise.
Bow down, bow down your face, I pray,
    To me, that swoon to death,
Breathe back the life you kissed away,
    Breathe back your kissing breath.
So by your eyes I swear and say,
    My mighty oath and sure,
From your kind arms no maiden may
    My loving heart allure.

I 'll bear your yoke, that 's light enough,
  And to the Elysian plain,
When we are dead of love, my love,
  One boat shall bear us twain.
They 'll flock around you, fleet and fair,
  All true loves that have been,
And you of all the shadows there,
  Shall be the shadow queen.
Ah shadow-loves, and shadow-lips!
  Ah, while 't is called to-day,
Love me, my love, for summer slips,
  And August ebbs away.

THE BURIAL OF MOLIÈRE.

(AFTER J. TRUFFIER.)

DEAD—he is dead! The rouge has left a trace
    On that thin cheek where shone, perchance, a tear,
  Even while the people laughed that held him dear
But yesterday. He died,—and not in grace,
And many a black-robed caitiff starts apace
    To slander him whose *Tartuffe* made them fear,
    And gold must win a passage for his bier,
And bribe the crowd that guards his resting-place.

Ah, Molière, for that last time of all,
  Man's hatred broke upon thee, and went by,
And did but make more fair thy funeral.
  Though in the dark they hid thee stealthily,
Thy coffin had the cope of night for pall,
  For torch, the stars along the windy sky!

BEFORE THE SNOW.

(AFTER ALBERT GLATIGNY.)

THE winter is upon us, not the snow,
  The hills are etched on the horizon bare,
The skies are iron grey, a bitter air,
The meagre cloudlets shudder to and fro.
One yellow leaf the listless wind doth blow,
  Like some strange butterfly, unclassed and rare.
  Your footsteps ring in frozen alleys, where
The black trees seem to shiver as you go.

Beyond lie church and steeple, with their old
  And rusty vanes that rattle as they veer,
A sharper gust would shake them from their hold.
  Yet up that path, in summer of the year,
And past that melancholy pile we strolled
  To pluck wild strawberries, with merry cheer.

THE CLOUD CHORUS.

(FROM ARISTOPHANES.)

Socrates speaks.

HITHER, come hither, ye Clouds renowned, and
unveil yourselves here;
Come, though ye dwell on the sacred crests of Olympian
snow,
Or whether ye dance with the Nereid choir in the
gardens clear,
Or whether your golden urns are dipped in Nile's overflow,
Or whether you dwell by Mæotis mere
Or the snows of Mimas, arise! appear!
And hearken to us, and accept our gifts ere ye rise and go.

The Clouds sing.

Immortal Clouds from the echoing shore
Of the father of streams, from the sounding sea,
Dewy and fleet, let us rise and soar.
Dewy and gleaming, and fleet are we!

Let us look on the tree-clad mountain crest,
  On the sacred earth where the fruits rejoice,
On the waters that murmur east and west,
  On the tumbling sea with his moaning voice.
For unwearied glitters the Eye of the Air,
  And the bright rays gleam ;
Then cast we our shadows of mist, and fare
In our deathless shapes to glance everywhere
    From the height of the heaven, on the land and air,
      And the Ocean stream.

Let us on, ye Maidens that bring the Rain,
  Let us gaze on Pallas' citadel,
    In the country of Cecrops, fair and dear
    The mystic land of the holy cell,
Where the Rites unspoken securely dwell,
  And the gifts of the Gods that know not stain
And a people of mortals that know not fear.
For the temples tall, and the statues fair,
And the feasts of the Gods are holiest there,
The feasts of Immortals, the chaplets of flowers
    And the Bromian mirth at the coming of spring,
And the musical voices that fill the hours,
    And the dancing feet of the Maids that sing !

www.ingramcontent.com/pod-product-compliance
Lightning Source LLC
Chambersburg PA
CBHW020542270326
41927CB00006B/689